Be the Best
BASKETBALL

Play Like a Pro
By James Allen

D1056860

Troll Associates

Library of Congress Cataloging-in-Publication Data

Allen, James, (date)
    Basketball, play like a pro / by James Allen.
        p.   cm.—(Be the best!)
    Summary: Explains basketball basics and provides drills and games
for improving different skills.
    ISBN 0-8167-1935-7 (lib. bdg.)   ISBN 0-8167-1936-5 (pbk.)
    1. Basketball—Juvenile literature.   [1. Basketball.]   I. Title.
II. Series.
    GV885.1.A43   1990
    796.323 '2—dc20   89-27351

Be the Best
BASKETBALL

Play Like a Pro

FOREWORD

by Wally Halas

Basketball is the world's greatest game. It is the only game I can think of that is always enjoyable whether played alone or with teammates, indoors or outdoors. And it can be played 365 days a year. To me, that's "basketball season"—all year long!

Basketball, Play Like a Pro, provides excellent basic instruction in how to play this greatest of all games. Read the book carefully. Then *practice* what you learn here. If you do, no matter what the final score may say, you'll be a winner in basketball. And you'll have great fun playing it besides.

Happy hoops!

Wally Halas

Wally Halas was the head basketball coach at Columbia University from the 1987-88 season through the 1989-90 season. Before coming to Columbia, Wally was the head basketball coach at Massachusetts' Clark University for 13 years. There, he coached the basketball team to 10 NCAA Division Three tournaments, resulting in 5 regional championships and 2 appearances in the overall championship final. Wally won 5 New England Coach of the Year Awards during that period. Besides coaching, Wally Halas was a star guard for Clark from 1969 to 1973. In his senior year, he was named team MVP and All-New England, and received the Bob Cousy Award as New England's best player under 6 feet in height.

Contents

The Story
Of Basketball

In the history of sports, basketball is like a new kid on
the block. It has not been around very long. Baseball,
soccer, and many other sports are much older. But
basketball has quickly become one of the most popular
sports in the world. It is loved by millions.

Before 1891 there was no basketball. The winter season
was often a boring time for athletes who liked competitive
games. At the YMCA Training School in Springfield,
Massachusetts, Dr. Luther Gulick wanted athletes to use
the gym during the winter. But the YMCA athletes were
tired of the old indoor activities. They wanted something
new and exciting to do.

Dr. Gulick told his assistant to make up a new indoor game. It could not be too rough and it had to be played in a small space. But most important of all, it had to be competitive and fun.

Dr. Gulick's assistant was a young Canadian who was a former athlete himself. He had been a gymnast and a football player at McGill University in Montreal. He knew a lot about sports. His name was Dr. James Naismith. Dr. Naismith is the Father of Basketball. The game he invented is now known as the sport of basketball.

How did basketball get its name? It was really by accident. Dr. Naismith decided his new game would be played with a large ball. Players would have to move around by bouncing the ball. But how could teams score points?

Dr. Naismith decided the ball should be shot into boxes hung at the opposite ends of the gym. But when he went to look for boxes, he couldn't find any. That was lucky. If he did, basketball might be known as boxball.

Instead, Dr. Naismith found empty peach baskets. He hooked them up ten feet high on the wall. Because of the peach baskets, the game was dubbed "basketball."

Using a soccer ball and the peach baskets, Dr. Naismith introduced basketball to athletes at Springfield in the winter of 1891. The game was an instant hit!

There was only one problem. Dr. Naismith did not remove the bottoms from the baskets. Every time a goal was scored, someone had to climb a ladder and get the ball out.

Nevertheless, the athletes at Springfield loved Dr. Naismith's new game. A list of thirteen basic rules was written. And a new winter sport was born!

When athletes left Springfield, they took the game of basketball with them. The sport soon spread throughout the United States and then the world.

In 1894, basketball was introduced in China and India. A year later, basketball was played in France, and Japan took up the sport in 1900. Soon colleges and schools all over the globe began to sponsor basketball teams. By 1913, basketball rules were printed in thirty different languages.

A truly American-made sport, basketball became an Olympic sport in 1936. Today, basketball is played in over 130 countries. Only soccer has more fans. People love basketball because it is thrilling to watch and easy to understand. Even learning about basketball is fun. Once you know all about the game, you will have even more fun playing it.

What You Need To Play Basketball

Do you need plenty of special equipment to play basketball? Not at all! Basketball players need practically no special equipment. They usually wear just shorts, sleeveless shirts, and sneakers.

Sometimes people play or practice basketball in regular street shoes. However, it is always best to wear sneakers. Buy the best sneakers you can afford if you are very serious about basketball. Make sure they fit right and provide strong ankle support.

The most important things you need for a basketball game are a basketball and a special place to play. That place must be a flat, level area. It can be inside a gym.

During warm weather, it can be outside at a school or playground. It can even be your own driveway or back yard. In basketball, that area is called a court. A court is usually in the shape of a rectangle, and has long side boundaries and shorter end boundaries.

At the ends of a basketball court are goals, although some games can be played with just one goal. A basketball goal is made up of two parts. One part is a flat, smooth backboard section. It is usually rectangular and made of wood, metal, or thick glass.

The second part is the goal itself, usually called the "basket." The goal is a circle of iron attached to the backboard. It is also called the hoop or the rim. It sticks out from the backboard so the ball can be shot through it. A net is attached on the bottom of the rim. (Some outdoor goals have no nets.) Basketball goals are always hung above the court. The ball must be shot up into them.

The object of a basketball game is to score more points than the other team. Points are scored by shooting the ball into the basket. Under normal conditions, each goal in basketball is worth two points. That is called a field goal.

A team starts at the end of the court opposite a goal. The ball is passed into the court from out of bounds (see page 57). The team then attempts to move the ball toward the goal. That team is on offense. Offense is when you have the ball.

The ball can be shot from anywhere on the court. But scoring is not easy in basketball. So an offensive team usually tries to get as close to the goal as it can.

If a shot at the goal is good, two points are scored and the other team gets the ball. It is then their turn to move toward the other goal.

If the shot misses, it is a free ball. The ball belongs to anyone who jumps up and grabs it. That is called a rebound. If the offense gets the rebound, the ball can be shot again. If the defense gets the rebound, the ball is dribbled or passed toward the opposite goal.

You can move the ball down the court by passing it to teammates. You can also advance the ball by bouncing it with your hand as you move. That is called dribbling. Only use one hand at a time. It is against the rules to carry or walk with the ball without dribbling. Once you stop dribbling, you must shoot or pass before you dribble again.

The other team is on defense. The defensive team tries to stop the advance of the ball or steal the ball away.

Rough play is not allowed. You cannot hold, push, trip, hit, or bump into an opposing player. Basketball is supposed to be a noncontact sport.

THE BASKETBALL

A regulation basketball is usually orange or tan and measures twenty-nine and a half to thirty inches around the middle. It weighs between twenty and twenty-two ounces. Occasionally you'll see red-white-and-blue basketballs being used.

A basketball for indoor play is made of leather with a rubber lining. A basketball for outdoor play is made of rubber. Rubber basketballs are made for dribbling on hard courts like playgrounds or driveways. Leather balls are used on indoor courts. Never use an indoor ball outside or you will damage it.

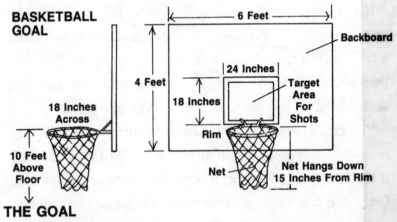

THE GOAL

The rim of an official basketball goal is ten feet above the floor of the basketball court. The mouth or ring part of the goal is eighteen inches across. The basket's net hangs down fifteen inches from the rim.

14

The backboard is usually a rectangle. (Backboards are also occasionally fan shaped.) The backboard measures four feet down and six feet across.

Another rectangle is painted in the middle of the backboard above the mouth of the basket. This smaller rectangle is twenty-four inches wide and eighteen inches high. It is there to form a target area for shots aimed at the backboard (see page 22).

THE COURT

Most indoor courts are waxed hardwood or tiled. Most outdoor courts are cement or macadam (also called blacktop). A basketball game, though, can be played anywhere there is a basketball goal. The size of the court is not important for neighborhood games.

However, a regulation basketball court is eighty-four to ninety-four feet long and fifty feet wide. The court is marked off with painted lines. The long ones are called sidelines. The shorter ones are called end lines. Another line cuts the court in half. It is called the mid-court line.

At the middle of the midcourt line are two circles, one inside the other. A regulation game begins there with a jump ball, which will be explained later (see page 55).

At each end of the court there is a smaller rectangular area and a circle. The long sides of the rectangle are called foul lanes. The short side of the rectangle nearest the midcourt line is called the foul line. The circle is called the foul circle.

BASKETBALL COURT

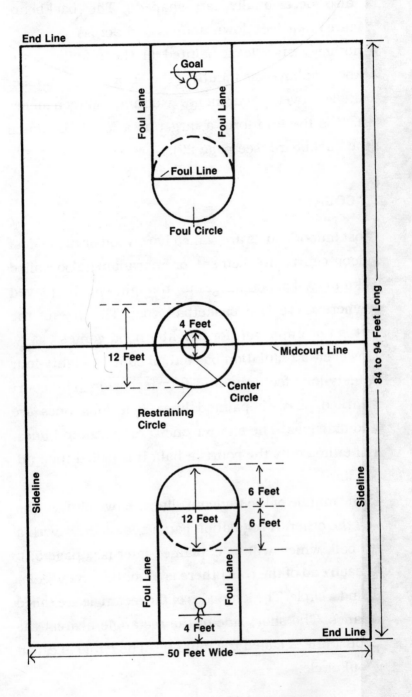

How to Develop
Basketball Skills

Basketball is a game of many skills. Some skills are physical and often cannot be taught or learned. There are no drills that make a short player tall, and it is hard for a poor jumper to become a great leaper.

But you can improve on the physical skills you already have. For example, a person who jumps well can be taught to jump better. And you can develop new skills, but that takes time. So do not get upset if your progress seems slow. Your physical skills may improve as you grow older. A good basketball player uses the skills he or she has and develops them to their fullest.

There are some parts of the game of basketball that can be taught and learned by everyone. They are called fundamentals. Learning them can be fun. You can learn to shoot, dribble, pass, rebound, and play defense the correct way. There are also drills that can sharpen those skills. So master the fundamentals if you want to play the game well.

STRETCHING

Before playing basketball, you should always stretch your muscles. Stretching helps prevent muscle pulls. One good stretch is done by sitting on the floor. Draw your feet toward your body, placing the soles or bottoms of your feet together. Your knees are out to the side. Hold your legs with your hands and slowly bend toward your feet.

STRETCHING

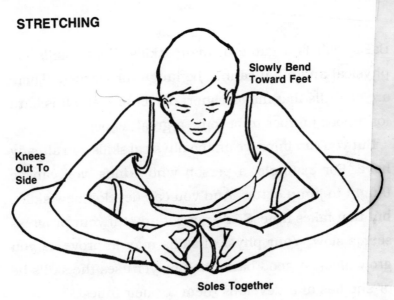

Slowly Bend Toward Feet

Knees Out To Side

Soles Together

PUSHUP

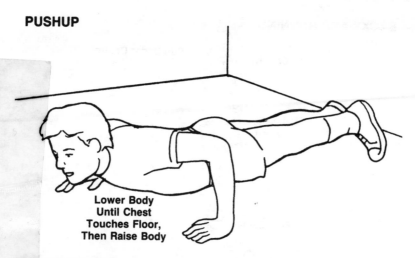

Lower Body
Until Chest
Touches Floor,
Then Raise Body

EXERCISING

Exercising before playing a game gets blood flowing to the muscles and warms them up. That helps prevent muscle cramps. Do several of your favorite exercises. Jumping jacks, sit-ups, pushups, squat thrusts, or any exercise can be used.

CONDITIONING

Basketball players have to run constantly. They need to be in good shape. The best way to develop stamina is to run laps or to combine laps with sprints.

Always try to be relaxed when you run, and breathe through your mouth and nose. Run on the balls of your feet, not your heels. At the beginning, never run too far. Stop when you feel tired. But always try to run a bit farther the next day. And remember to run at a steady rate, pacing yourself. The exception is running sprints, which you should try to do at full speed or close to it.

19

BACKWARD RUNNING

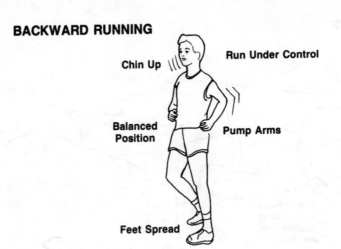

Chin Up

Run Under Control

Balanced Position

Pump Arms

Feet Spread

BACKWARD RUNNING

Defensive play requires basketball players to move backwards while guarding an opponent. Practice running or moving quickly backwards. When running backwards, keep your feet spread or you will trip over your own feet. Lean slightly forward in a balanced position. Pump your arms. And keep your chin up. When practicing running backwards, always run under control so you don't bump into anything or anyone.

JUMPING

When you jump, always have your feet spread. That gives you a good base to take off from. Bend your knees, keeping your weight on the front of your feet. As you leap, use your arms to catapult yourself upward. Always stretch out your body and arms as far as you can.

Try to develop spring in your legs by jumping several times rapidly. Go up-down-up-down-up-down!

20

Shooting the
Basketball

When you throw the ball toward the hoop and try to
make it go in, that is a shot. Making a successful shot
is not easy. To become a good scorer, you must practice
a shot properly. There are many different shots in basketball. Practice them all. The more shots you develop,
the better a player you will be.

Whenever you shoot, always try to face the hoop.
Have the ball under control. Keep the fingers on your
shooting hand spread to control the ball better. Do not
just throw the ball toward the hoop. Aim at the basket
and concentrate on your target. Then, follow through.
That means when the ball leaves your hand, let the
motion of your hand continue so you actually wave
goodbye to the ball. That also gives the ball backspin.

BANKING A SHOT

BANK SHOT

Not all shots are aimed right at the basket. Some shots use the backboard. The ball bounces off the backboard into the basket. That is called a bank shot. The tiny rectangle painted behind the basket is a target for bank shots. If you hit that target at the proper angle and have the right spin and speed on the ball, it should go in the hoop.

Bank shots are especially good to use when you are off to the side of the basket. Knowing how to bank the ball in is a great offensive weapon.

LAY-UP

The lay-up is the shot to use when you can move or drive unguarded toward the basket. It is a simple shot every player should master.

To do a lay-up, a right-handed player should move toward the basket on an angle from the right side. (The opposite is true for a left-handed player.) When you are close to the basket, raise your right foot and push off with your left foot. Jump for height, not distance. Hold the ball in two hands as you go up. Keep your eyes on your target. Then reach up with one hand and gently lay the ball against the backboard so it will bounce off into the basket.

LAY-UP SHOT

Soft Shot
Off Backboard With
One Hand

Ball In
Two Hands

Right
Leg Up

3.

Dribble In
From Side

Push Off
With
Left Foot

1.

2.

There are several keys to doing a lay-up properly. Time your jump so you are not too far under the basket. Have a soft touch as you lay the ball off the backboard. If you do it too hard, the ball will bounce over the rim. Keep your eyes on the target. Do not just throw the ball up and hope it will go in.

Lay-ups can be practiced by standing close to the side of the basket. Jump up and lay the ball in off the backboard. Once you master that, try taking a two-step drive in. Concentrate on pushing off on the correct foot: right foot from the left side, left foot from the right side.

After mastering a lay-up from one side, practice driving from the other side. It will be hard but it will make you a better player.

LEFT-HANDED LAY-IN

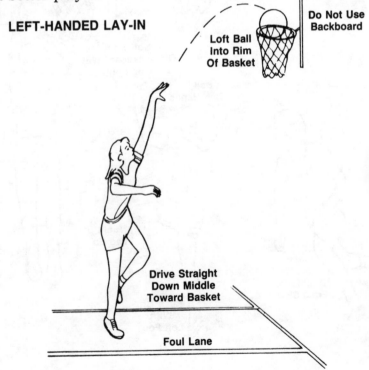

Do Not Use
Backboard

Loft Ball
Into Rim
Of Basket

Drive Straight
Down Middle
Toward Basket

Foul Lane

LAY-IN

Another kind of lay-up is called a lay-in. To do a lay-in, you drive straight down the middle of the foul line and toward the basket. Remember, you do not approach from the side. You go straight in. For a lay-in, do not use the backboard. Gently loft the ball over the front rim into the basket.

JUMP SHOT

The jump shot is very difficult to defend against when it is done correctly. It is the favorite shot of most high-school, college, and pro players.

The jump shot is a one-handed shot combined with a jump. The ball is released at the peak or height of the jump. While shooting, the player seems to hang in the air for a second. It is a beautiful shot to watch.

If you are right-handed, your right hand will be the shooting hand and it will control the ball. The left hand provides support and balance. The shooting hand should be on the middle of the basketball to the back. Keep your fingers spread. The ball rests on the fingertips and upper part of the hand. The fingertips of the left hand are on the side of the ball toward the back. Your shooting elbow is tucked into your body.

As you prepare to take your jump shot, focus on your target. Hold the ball about chin high, looking over it. Spread your feet, bend your knees, and start your jump. When you reach the highest point of the jump, fire the

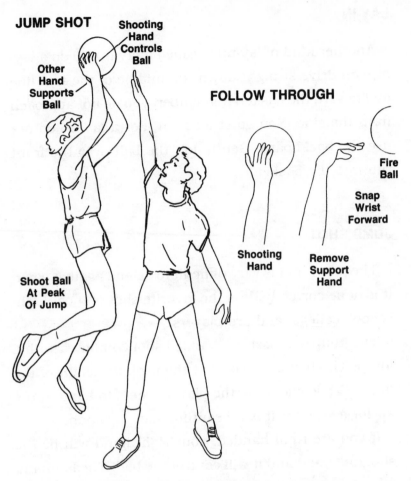

JUMP SHOT

Shooting Hand Controls Ball

Other Hand Supports Ball

Shoot Ball At Peak Of Jump

FOLLOW THROUGH

Fire Ball

Snap Wrist Forward

Shooting Hand

Remove Support Hand

ball. If you shoot too soon or too late, your shot may not stay on course.

To shoot, raise the ball over your head and extend your shooting arm, pushing the ball away from you. Remove the support hand. As you fire, the middle three fingers of your shooting hand provide most of the push. The middle and index fingertips of that hand should be the last thing to touch the ball as it sails away.

Follow through by snapping your wrist forward. That is your goodbye wave to the shot.

HOOK SHOT

The hook shot is exciting to watch. But it is a very difficult shot to master, especially for beginners. So do not be upset if you cannot make a hook shot. It takes lots and lots of practice to do it right.

The hook shot is a one-handed shot. It is done by firing the ball over your head with a sweeping motion of the arm. In this shot, your body does not face the basket. You take the shot from a sideways position.

In the hook shot, more of the hand touches the ball than with any other shot. Your fingers really have to be spread for good control. As you shoot, concentrate on the basket. Lift the leg on the side of your shooting hand. Push off with the other leg. While in the air,

HOOK SHOT

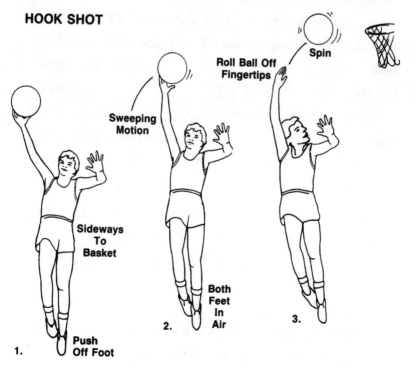

Sweeping Motion

Roll Ball Off Fingertips

Spin

Sideways To Basket

Both Feet In Air

Push Off Foot

1.

2.

3.

27

deliver the ball over your head in a hooking motion toward the hoop. Release the ball when your arm is extended straight over your head. Remember to let it roll off your fingertips. Proper spin is important in a hook shot.

When taking hook shots from the side of the basket, try banking the ball in. Again, a hook shot is not a good shot for beginners. And even many pros use it only once in a while during a game.

ONE-HANDED PUSH SHOT

Also called the set shot, the push shot was the most common shot in basketball before the jump shot came along. Today, when the one-handed push shot is used, the player is usually unguarded and shooting from a long distance. But it is still a shot that can come in handy.

For the one-handed push shot, hold the ball in two hands with one underneath and one on the side for guiding. Use mostly your fingertips. The ball should *not* rest on your palms.

Face the basket. Spread your feet about shoulder width. Stay balanced, keeping your weight on the balls of your feet. Hold the ball out about nose high from your body. You should be able to look over the ball at the basket. Keep your elbows in.

Focus your eyes on a spot just over the rim. That is your target. Bend your knees slightly. Draw the ball

ONE-HANDED PUSH SHOT

toward you and up over your forehead. Push forward with your arms and snap your wrist as you release the ball. Let the ball roll off your fingertips. Straighten your knees and rise up on your toes.

FOUL SHOOTING

At times during a regulation game, players get a free shot. The shot is called a foul shot. A foul shot is awarded when the other team breaks certain rules. (More about this will be discussed under "Fouls" on pages 58-60.)

A foul shot is taken from the foul line, which is fifteen feet from the basket. A player can have one or two foul shots, depending on which rule has been broken and how. Each foul shot made is worth one point.

FOUL SHOOTING

**Both Feet
Behind
Foul Line**

Before taking a foul shot, make sure both of your feet are behind the foul line. If you step on it or over it, the shot will not count. Try to use the same shot for all your foul shots. Stay in the same spot and position.

It is important to be relaxed at the foul line. Bounce the ball. Take a breath. Stand with your feet apart and aim at your target. That target is just over the front rim.

Most players today use a modified jump shot for a foul shot. Bend deep at the knees. Position your hands as in the jump shot. But start your shot lower—near chest level. Bring the ball upward to eye level in one easy motion. When it reaches eye level or slightly above, straighten your knees and release the ball.

This sounds like a whole bunch of things to do but they should all be done in one continuous motion. Always remember to follow through. Shoot softly so you develop a shooter's touch. Sometimes softer shots that are slightly off the mark will fall in. Practice your foul shots as often as you can.

Dribbling

Dribbling is pushing the ball against the floor in a series of controlled bounces. The key word is *control*. A good dribbler always has control of the ball.

The first thing to learn about dribbling is the position of the hand on the ball. You *cannot* touch the ball with two hands at the same time while dribbling. But you *can* switch from one hand to the other.

To dribble, keep your fingers spread. But do not spread them so far that they feel stiff or rigid. They should feel relaxed. Use the fingers and fingertips to dribble. Do not slap at the ball with your palms.

Dribble in a crouched position with your knees bent. When dribbling, do not let the ball bounce too high. Bounces should be kept at waist level.

DRIBBLING

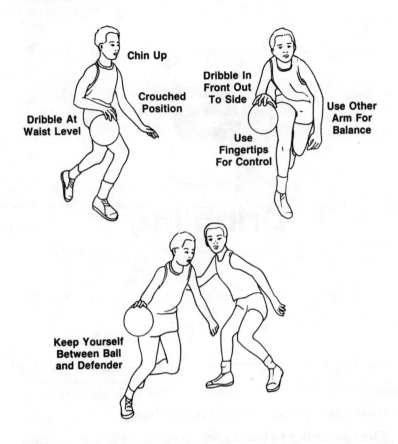

Chin Up

Dribble In
Front Out
To Side

Crouched
Position

Use Other
Arm For
Balance

Dribble At
Waist Level

Use
Fingertips
For Control

Keep Yourself
Between Ball
and Defender

Do not stare at the ball as you bounce it. Keep your chin up and try to look straight ahead. That way, you will develop a feel for the ball, and be able to spot an open teammate to pass to. You will also protect the ball better from the defense. Dribble out in front of you and slightly to the side. Keep your free arm out for balance.

Learn to dribble with either hand. When dribbling past an opponent, keep your body between the ball and your opponent. As your dribbling improves, change speeds, hands, and direction.

Rebounding

Getting the ball after a missed shot is called a rebound. Rebounding the ball is very important in basketball.

A tall player has a big advantage when it comes to rebounding. But shorter players can be good rebounders too. There are several keys to being a good rebounder.

Being in the right place at the right time can help you get a lot of rebounds. After you shoot the ball, do not stand around and watch it. Follow your shot toward the basket. If you miss, you might get the rebound. If you see someone else shooting, move toward the basket. Try to slip in front of your opponents. But do not push, shove, or trip. That is against the rules. If an opponent is behind you, use your body to stay between him or her and the basket. That is called boxing out.

33

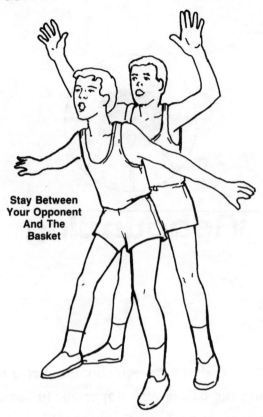

**Stay Between
Your Opponent
And The
Basket**

When going up for a rebound, jump as high as you can and stretch as far as you can. Do not be afraid. There is more contact during rebounding than in any other part of the game of basketball. A good rebounder must be tough and aggressive.

Time your jump when you go up for a rebound. When you grab the ball, hold it tightly. When you come down, land on the balls of your feet. Keep your elbows up and pointed out to the sides to protect yourself. Hold the ball about chest level or higher. Pass the ball to a teammate or dribble as soon as it is safe to do so.

Passing

CHEST PASS

The chest pass is a straight, sharp pass. It is used when there is a clear path between you and the person you want to pass to. To make a chest pass, place your hands on the sides of the ball near the back. The thumbs should be almost touching each other.

People who really know basketball know a good passer helps make a team go. If you pass the ball to someone who makes a basket, you get credit for an assist. Getting an assist in basketball is almost as good as scoring. Players who make a lot of assists are stars in their own right. So don't try to shoot all the time. Learn how to pass. Become a star passer and get lots of assists!

CHEST PASS

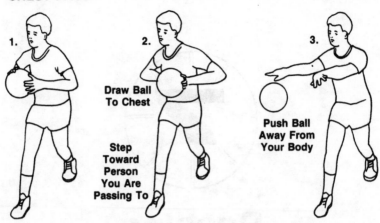

1.

2.

**Draw Ball
To Chest**

**Step
Toward
Person
You Are
Passing To**

3.

**Push Ball
Away From
Your Body**

The pass is called a chest pass because that is where it starts. The ball is held chest high and should almost touch your chest. Elbows are up and pointed out.

Look at the person you are passing to. Step toward him or her. Push the ball away from your body as you step. Do not throw the ball. As you push, snap your wrists sharply. That gives the pass its speed.

BOUNCE PASS

The motion of the bounce pass is just like the chest pass. There is one big difference. You do not pass the ball directly in the air to your teammate. The ball is bounced off the floor to your teammate.

A bounce pass is used when an opponent is between you and the person you want to pass to. If you threw a chest pass, it would probably be intercepted. It is very difficult to intercept a bounce pass that is done correctly. It should be done on either side of the opponent, *not* through his or her legs.

Hold the ball the same way you did for the chest pass. Start the pass from the chest level or slightly lower. Do not raise the ball over your shoulders or head. Concentrate on a spot on the floor. It should be about two-thirds the distance between you and the person you are passing to. You want to get the ball to your teammate on one bounce. That bounce should reach him or her when it is about waist high. Step and push the ball away. Aim at the spot you picked on the floor.

A bounce pass is a good pass to use when a teammate is moving toward the basket unguarded. But remember to lead him or her with the pass. That means delivering the ball far enough in front of your teammate so that he or she can catch it without breaking stride or reaching back.

BOUNCE PASS

Aim At A Spot On The Floor

Bounce Ball Off Floor To Your Teammate

Ball Reaches Teammate At Waist Level

BASEBALL PASS

You want to throw the basketball a long way down court in a hurry. Which pass should you use? The answer is the baseball pass.

A baseball pass is thrown with one hand. It's like the throw of a baseball catcher to second base. The ball is held in one hand. The arm is bent with the ball just behind the ear. The passer steps and throws.

This pass should be used only when a teammate is open at the opposite end of the court. Otherwise, it is easy to intercept.

BASEBALL PASS

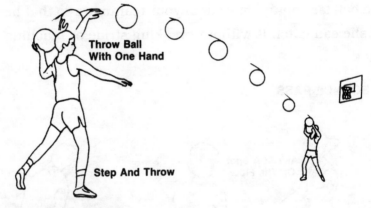

Throw Ball With One Hand

Step And Throw

OVERHEAD PASS

You can use the overhead pass to arch the ball over the outstretched hands of the defense. Make sure the pass is high and accurate enough to avoid interception.

In the overhead pass, the ball is held with two hands over the head. The grip is the same one used for the chest pass. Bend your arms at the elbows and then snap them forward as you throw the ball. The key is not to get the ball too far behind your head.

Playing Defense

When most people think of basketball, they think of offense. They think of scoring and assists. However, defense is a big part of the game. Playing good defense can win you a place on a team. A complete basketball player is good on offense and defense.

DEFENSIVE POSITION

To play defense, you must be in a ready position. From a ready position you can quickly move in any direction.

To start, spread your feet about shoulder width or a bit wider. Bend your knees, turning them slightly outward. Keeping your back straight, lean slightly forward while lowering your seat. Stretch out your arms.

Your right arm should be out in front to the right, with the palm up and fingers spread. Your left arm should be out to the side. Spread your arms for balance.

That is the position to be in when a player is dribbling toward you from the right. If a player dribbles toward you from the left, switch the positions of your arms.

DEFENSIVE POSITION

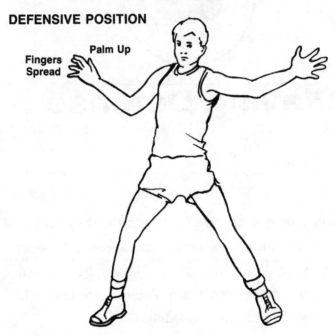

Palm Up

Fingers
Spread

PLAYER-TO-PLAYER DEFENSE

Player-to-player defense means each defensive player guards one member of the opposite team. The defensive player stays with the person he or she is assigned to guard.

Tall players usually match up against tall players. Quick players match up against quick players, and so on. The key to player-to-player defense is getting the right match-ups.

PLAYER-TO-PLAYER DEFENSE

Each defensive player will guard one opponent

When you are in a player-to-player defense, stay with the person you are supposed to guard. Do not let him or her get behind you. Try to stay between your player and the basket. Do not let him or her get an open shot if you can help it.

Also, communicate with your teammates. If you see something they can't, tell them right away. This will help prevent any lapses in player-to-player defending.

ZONE DEFENSE

Zone defense means you stay in an area close to the basket. Each player is assigned an area or a zone to guard. If a person comes into your area, then you must guard him or her. If he or she leaves your area, that player is no longer your responsibility. The key to zone defense is staying where you belong. Do not leave your zone unguarded. (Zone defense is not permitted in the N.B.A.)

ZONE DEFENSE

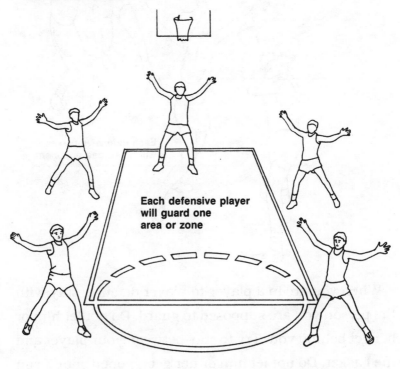

Each defensive player will guard one area or zone

Dribbling and Passing Drills

There's no substitute for practice. You can get the practice you need in dribbling and passing through drills designed to improve these two basic basketball skills. A few of the more popular ones follow.

SWITCHING YOUR DRIBBLE HAND

A good way to practice dribbling is to dribble down court using one hand and to dribble back with the other. Go slowly the first few times. Then try to dribble for speed.

Another way to practice is to change hands with each dribble. Dribble right to left, left to right, and so on. (See pages 31-32 for more on dribbling.)

DRIBBLING AROUND CONES

This next dribbling drill will help you develop ball control while changing direction. The object is to dribble around cones, cups, or anything that can be placed on the floor of the court. Dribble between and around each cone, weaving between them.

DRIBBLING AROUND CONES

To make the drill harder, keep your body between the cone and the ball. When you go around a cone to the right, dribble with your right hand. As you weave around the next cone to your left, use your left hand. Pretend the cones are defenders.

PRACTICE GAMES IMPROVE PASSING

Passing is difficult to practice alone. You can practice against a wall, but that does not give you the timing you need to be a good passer.

The best way to practice passing is to play a lot of two-on-two or three-on-three games. In those games, you must pass frequently.

**THREE-ON-THREE GAME
TO IMPROVE PASSING**

PASSING WITH A PARTNER

By using a partner, you can stand facing each other on opposite foul lanes. From there you can practice a bounce pass, a chest pass, or an overhead pass.

PASS SHUFFLE

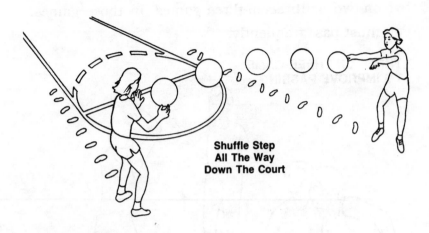

**Shuffle Step
All The Way
Down The Court**

PASS SHUFFLE

Another way to practice passing is to start facing each other on opposite foul lanes. Throw chest passes back and forth as you shuffle step or sidestep all the way down the court. This means you face each other and move sideways down court. When you reach the basket, one player takes a shot. Remember not to cross your legs as you move.

Shooting Drills
And Games

The best way to improve shooting is to practice it as often as you can. When practicing, try a variety of shots. Do a lay-up, a jump shot, a bank shot, a hook shot, or any combination. Some players practice shots in combinations until they make each one.

Other players practice shooting from special places on the court. They don't move from one spot to the next until they make, or sink, a basket.

As you shoot around, you will develop favorite shots. You will also find areas or spots on the court where you can score more easily. That is what players are talking about when they refer to *their* shot or *their* spot.

AROUND-THE-WORLD GAME

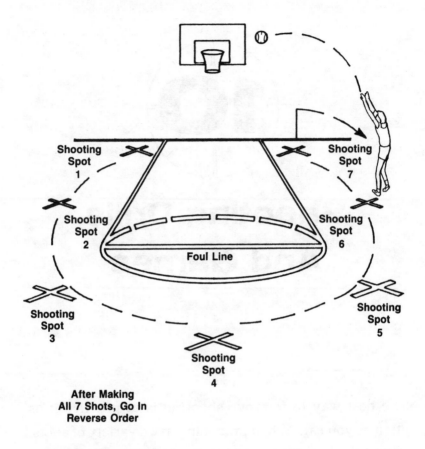

Shooting Spot 1

Shooting Spot 2

Shooting Spot 3

Foul Line

Shooting Spot 4

Shooting Spot 5

Shooting Spot 6

Shooting Spot 7

After Making
All 7 Shots, Go In
Reverse Order

AROUND THE WORLD

"Around the World" is a shooting game you can play alone or with friends. The object is to make baskets from several different spots on the court. Usually the first spot is very near one side of the basket on the foul lane. Two more spots are picked between the first spot and the foul line. The foul line is always the midway spot. On the other foul lane, pick three more shooting spots directly across from the first three.

48

The idea is to make a basket at each spot. Once you make it, move onto the next spot. After you go all around the seven spots, go in reverse, shooting from each spot again until you reach spot one. End by making three shots in a row from the foul line.

If you're playing with friends, each person takes a turn. You shoot until you miss. If you miss, you stay at the spot you missed from until your next turn. The first one to shoot all "around the world" wins.

H-O-R-S-E

"H-O-R-S-E" is a simple shooting game that can be played with two or more players.

One player takes a shot. If he or she makes it, then player two must make the same shot from the same spot. For example, if player one makes a hook shot from the foul line, player two must make a hook shot from the foul line. If player two misses the shot, he or she gets a letter . . . H.

A GAME OF H-O-R-S-E

YOU GET AN ..."E"!
THAT SPELLS..."HORSE"!
I WIN!

THUNK!

If player two makes the shot, he or she does not get a letter. Player one goes again. If player one misses, player two gets to shoot any shot he or she likes. If player two scores a basket, player one must duplicate the shot. Otherwise, player one gets a letter.

Play continues with letters building up. If a player's letters spell "H-O-R-S-E," he or she is out. The other player wins.

ONE-ON-ONE

"One-on-One" is like a real basketball game between two players. It pits one person against another. It sharpens dribbling, shooting, rebounding, and defensive skills.

To play, you only need part of a basketball court. The ball is started from behind the foul line near one basket. (See the diagram on page 16.) One player tries to score against the other. If the defensive player gets the ball, he or she takes it back behind the foul line before turning around and trying to score at the same basket.

Sometimes a special rule is used in this game. If a shot does not hit the rim, the defensive player does not have to dribble to the foul line before going on offense. He or she can take the ball in for a shot.

You can expand this "One-on-One" game to a "Two-on-Two" or even a "Three-on-Three" game with more players.

TWENTY-ONE

"Twenty-One" is a basketball game similar to "One-on-One." "Twenty-One" is often played when the sides are uneven. For example, five people want to play. One player gets the ball behind the foul line and starts on offense. The other four are all on defense. Each player is his or her own team. A field goal (see page 13) is worth two points. Any player who makes a field goal goes to the foul line. He or she has the opportunity to make three foul shots worth one point each. It is possible to make a total of five points. If a player makes a field goal and all three foul shots, the ball still belongs to that player. He or she begins again on offense behind the foul line.

If that player misses any of those shots (the field-goal try or any of the three foul shots), it is a free ball. The ball belongs to anyone who gets the rebound. It can be shot immediately. It does not have to be returned to the foul line. That's how the game is played.

Each player keeps track of his or her own points (two each for a field goal, one for each foul shot). The first player to score twenty-one points wins the game.

Positions

On the court, a basketball team is made up of five players. There are two guards, two forwards, and one center.

GUARDS

Guards are usually the smallest players on a team. They are also usually the quickest players and the best dribblers. Guards set up plays and run the offense. They are good passers. A *shooting* guard is usually the better scorer of the two. He or she drives in for lay-ups and takes outside shots. A *point* guard will handle the ball most of the time. He or she does more of the passing and helps create plays for teammates. A point guard does not often drive toward the basket unless there's a clear path to it. The point guard is usually a good defensive player too.

BASKETBALL POSITIONS

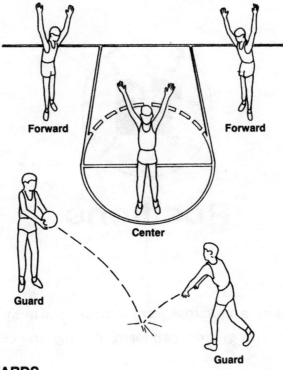

Forward

Forward

Center

Guard

Guard

FORWARDS

Forwards are usually tall players who position themselves out near the sides of the basket. They must be good rebounders. Forwards can also handle the ball well. They know how to drive in for lay-ups. They can also shoot from the outside.

CENTER

The center is usually the tallest player. He or she plays in the middle on offense and defense. A center's job is to block shots and rebound. Usually the center is a good scorer when close to the basket.

Regulation Play

JUMP BALL

A regulation game is started with a jump ball. A player from each team stands in the center circle at midcourt (see pages 15-16). One foot of each player must be in the smaller circle. All other players stand outside the larger circle.

The referee throws the ball straight up between the two players. They jump for the ball but cannot grab it. They must tap it to a teammate. The team that gets it has possession.

Until recently a jump ball was called by a referee when he or she couldn't tell which team the ball belonged to during play. That's why there are jump circles

JUMP BALL

near both foul lines. Now, however, a new possession rule exists in high-school and college basketball. After the game-opening jump ball, teams take turns getting the basketball instead of jumping for it. This is usually indicated at the scorer's table by an arrow lit in the direction of team possession.

OUT-OF-BOUNDS PLAY

After scoring plays or after play has stopped, the ball must be taken out of bounds. That means the ball starts outside the rectangular boundary of the court and must be passed in to a player on the court.

Depending on the situation, the ball may be passed in from the end line or the sideline. It is not a free pass. The other team can intercept the pass in. There is also a time limit. A team has five seconds to pass the ball in. If they can't, the other team gets the ball.

Once the ball is passed inbounds after a change of possession, the offensive team has ten seconds to get it across the midcourt line. If they can't, the other team gets the ball.

BALL BEING PASSED IN

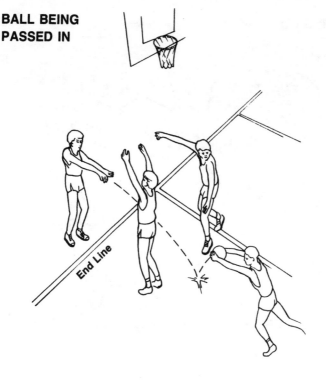

End Line

FOULS

Fouls are sometimes difficult to explain and understand. They are even harder to call during a game. But they are an important part of basketball. Fouls keep basketball games from getting too rough.

Personal Fouls These are called when a player pushes, holds, hits, trips, or runs into a member of the opposite team.

A record is kept of how many fouls each player commits during a game. If a player commits five personal fouls, he or she fouls out and can no longer play in that game. (In professional basketball, a player fouls out after committing six fouls.)

FOULING OUT

If a player is shooting while fouled, that player is given foul shots (see page 29). Foul shots are free shots taken from the foul line (see page 15). A player fouled while shooting gets two foul shots.

If the player fouled while shooting still manages to score, the basket counts. He or she then gets only one foul shot. A field goal and a made foul shot are sometimes called a three-point play.

THREE-POINT PLAY...FOULED WHILE SHOOTING

Not every foul results in a free throw. If the person fouled is not shooting or does not have the ball, there are no free shots. Play is stopped and the ball is inbounded by the fouled player's team.

Sometimes free throws are awarded even if a player is not shooting. It is a special case, depending on how many team fouls the guilty team has.

Team Fouls These are fouls charged against all the players on one team. If the fouls of all the players of one team add up to five, that team has reached its allowed limit for a half.

If a team is over the limit when they foul, the player fouled gets to shoot special foul shots. These are called one and one. The player fouled gets one shot. If the player misses, that's all he or she gets. If the shot is good, the player is entitled to a second shot. In order to get two shots in a one and one, you have to make the first one.

Technical Fouls   These are mostly called for unsportsmanlike conduct. This can include one player fighting or dangerously fouling another, or a coach or player using profanity while speaking to a referee during the game. A technical foul is a one- or two-shot foul depending on the offense. The team shooting the foul shot gets to keep the ball on offense.

TECHNICAL FOUL

VIOLATIONS

A violation is breaking a basic rule of basketball. When a team commits a violation, possession of the ball is awarded to the other team. These violations include:

Traveling   This violation occurs when a player with the basketball takes steps without dribbling or takes extra steps when shooting or driving for a lay-up.

TRAVELING VIOLATION

Three-Second Violation   When a player on offense stays between the foul lanes under the basket for more than three seconds, a three-second violation is called. Offensive players must move in and out of that area. They cannot stay right under the basket for longer than three seconds.

Double Dribble   When a player bounces the ball with two hands at the same time, he or she has committed a double dribble. Another double-dribble violation is to stop dribbling and then dribble again.

Palming   This is called when a player's dribbling hand touches the underside of the ball for too long.

Back-Court Violation   Beginners frequently commit this violation. Once a team moves the ball across the midcourt line, they cannot take the ball back across that line unless the ball is first touched by a defender.

Kicking   You can neither intentionally kick the basketball nor strike it with your fist. Both are violations.

KICKING THE BALL—A VIOLATION

Sportsmanship

Basketball is a great game to watch and play. It is even more fun to play if you play the game right. Develop good teamwork. Do not shoot every time you touch the ball. Always hustle during a game. Don't complain or argue. Play by the rules and try not to foul. If you have a coach, listen to him or her. You may not become a superstar player, but good sportsmanship can make you a superstar person.

INDEX